TRAUMA RECOVERY JOURNAL

Trauma Recovery
JOURNAL

Reflective Prompts and
Evidence-Based Practices
to Help You Recover,
Heal, and Thrive

Trudy Gilbert-Eliot, PhD, LMFT, LCADC

callisto
publishing
an imprint of Sourcebooks

Copyright © 2021 by Callisto Publishing LLC
Cover and internal design © 2021 by Callisto Publishing LLC
Illustrations: Courtesy of Basia Stryjecka/Creative Market
Interior and Cover Designer: Alan Carr
Art Producer: Janice Ackerman
Editor: John Makowski
Production Editor: Jax Berman
Production Manager: Martin Worthington

Published by Callisto Publishing LLC C/O Sourcebooks LLC
P.O. Box 4410, Naperville, Illinois 60567-4410
(630) 961-3900
callistopublishing.com

Printed and bound in China
OGP 2

This journal belongs to:

....

CONTENTS

Introduction   ix

How to Use Your Journal   xi

SECTION 1: START WHERE YOU ARE   1

SECTION 2: THOUGHTS, FEELINGS, AND SENSATIONS 51

SECTION 3: HEALTHY BODY AND MIND   87

SECTION 4: GROWING AND THRIVING   121

Resources   155

References   158

INTRODUCTION

Welcome to a journaling experience that will bring you insight and deep awareness about how trauma has impacted your life. I'm Trudy Gilbert-Eliot, and I've specialized in treating trauma for over 20 years. In my practice as a psychotherapist, I've worked with survivors of a wide variety of traumas, including domestic violence, childhood sexual abuse, sexual assault, and trauma related to mass shootings and to military, law enforcement, and firefighter service.

After my involvement in treating survivors of the 2017 mass shooting in Las Vegas, I witnessed the importance of having as many tools as possible to overcome the effects of trauma. Discovering the combination of interventions that works best for you will be part of your recovery journey.

Trauma can be defined as any event that exceeds or crushes your coping abilities. Only a very small subset of people who experience trauma will end up with the clinical condition called post-traumatic stress disorder (PTSD). However, *everyone* who experiences a traumatic event must address the effects and build their coping resources back up to full strength.

Trauma can have many different causes. The ones most people are familiar with involve events such as car accidents, being robbed, and being assaulted. But trauma can also be experienced when you're bullied at school or work, if you undergo repeated medical interventions for a chronic illness, or from the ongoing effects of systemic racism. As this book is being written, the world is dealing with the collective trauma of the global COVID-19 pandemic. These traumas are all different, and the symptoms look extremely different from person to person. Throughout this journal, you will learn to explore the symptoms that are unique to your experience, and together we will work to understand and overcome them.

Why a journal? Journaling has been found to help people work through their problems, reduce stress, gain perspective, notice patterns, and achieve goals. In an interesting research study from 2006, participants were encouraged to either write or draw about a stressful experience twice a week. The researchers found that those who wrote about their experiences had more significant reductions in their distressing symptoms compared to those who were assigned to the drawing group. Journaling can be a powerful tool to help you cope with your experiences, process difficult emotions, and much more.

My hope for you is that the various exercises and practices described in this book will help you better understand and manage your trauma symptoms. The pages of your journal will be a safe place to explore, reflect, document, and gain support on your healing journey.

HOW TO USE YOUR JOURNAL

This book is comprised of four sections. Within each, you'll find a mix of four components that will help direct you in your exploration.

First, each section is titled after a **theme**. Each theme describes a different way of interacting with your trauma responses, and each section includes a discussion to explore how you've been personally impacted by trauma.

Second, the **journaling prompts** include rich questions related to the theme, encouraging you to write about your experiences in as much depth as you would like. Prompts may ask you to describe an experience in detail, project how you would like to feel in the future, or set intentions to work on specific aspects of your thinking, feeling, or behavior. Some prompts will repeat in order to provide you with as much space as possible to reflect on how your trauma has impacted you.

Along with that, we'll offer some **practices** to empower you to feel better and gain more traction in the recovery process. These practices are new skills you can develop, activities to try out, and healthy new routines to utilize in order to gain more understanding of yourself.

Along the way, **affirmations** that relate to each theme will provide you with anchoring statements that remind you about your goals relating to recovery. Repeat your favorite affirmations daily, several times a day, or whenever you need to counter negative thinking, self-criticism, or stress. You can say them out loud or silently in your mind, whichever feels best. It's also helpful to write them on sticky notes and place them where you'll see them: on a bathroom mirror, in your car, or on the back of your phone.

Your journal can be used in a very flexible manner. You may want to complete each prompt and practice in order, from the beginning of the book to the end. Another option is to address the topics that are most difficult for you first, in order to get immediate relief. Perhaps you'll decide to only write in your journal when your symptoms feel difficult to manage.

Journaling is a very personal experience, and there is no right or wrong way to do it. It may be useful to find a quiet place and write at the same time each day. Some people prefer bullet points, while others write in a narrative style. Relax and write whatever comes to mind. Avoid self-judgment about what you are writing, or things like spelling or phrasing. This journal is for you, not for anyone else. You can regularly review sections and add new information as you gain insight and understanding.

A guided journal practice can be a powerful way to work through trauma symptoms. But do keep in mind that this can never be a replacement for professional help if you have severe or ongoing symptoms of anxiety, depression, or PTSD. If your symptoms frequently feel unmanageable, it's imperative you seek help from a medical professional to be properly diagnosed and begin treatment. It's also possible that as you become more self-aware through journaling, you may conclude that seeking professional help would be a courageous act of self-care.

Now, shall we get on to the real work? I'm excited that you have decided to take this journey!

Start Where You Are

Some journeys are long, twisty, and difficult. Others are brief, straightforward, and clear. No matter what type of voyage you undertake, it's always necessary to determine your starting point first. To increase your focus on this first task, in this chapter we'll explore three separate indicators of your starting point.

Naming your trauma can be an essential step in knowing the direction your recovery must take. Experiences that fit under the definition of trauma have a very wide range, and include physical, emotional, psychological, and neglectful components. If you're in any way uncomfortable writing about abuse you've suffered, keep to a general level when writing or thinking about your trauma. You may wish to return later and add more detail.

Beginning to articulate your symptoms, including how you feel about yourself, is the next important task to clarify where you are right now. Trauma symptoms that you've experienced for years may be difficult to identify, because we all adjust and adapt to cope with life. Trauma also changes how we view ourselves: our self-definition, our self-worth, and our beliefs about our future can all be affected. Learning how these aspects of trauma have shaped us can allow us to know what steps we must take next.

Once you have clarity about your trauma and your current symptoms, you will find that **determining your goals** can easily flow from the perspective you've gained. Having a long-term goal can help you find the first, most necessary direction to begin your journey toward healing.

I can become comfortable with exploring my symptoms in order to forge a path to overcome them. Awareness is the key to growth. I will strive to be open and nonjudgmental.

Learn Some Basic Mindfulness

Mindfulness can help us be more accepting of reality, decrease judgment of ourselves and others, and become more effective in each moment. Simply put, mindfulness draws our attention to the present moment. Here are three steps to core mindfulness that you can use to bring mindfulness into your life whenever you need to:

1. **Observe.** When you observe yourself feeling sad, you will notice much more than if you are absorbed in sadness.

2. **Describe.** Use words to illustrate your thoughts, feelings, sensations, or physical reactions. Use nonjudgmental statements like "I am feeling sadness in waves," instead of "I'm too weak to handle this sadness."

3. **Participate.** Become fully engaged in whatever activity you're involved in. What are you seeing, hearing, and tasting?

Mindfulness exercises can be very useful when you feel intense emotions while journaling, and as a general stress reliever. Practice mindfulness regularly in order to have the skill at your disposal when you most need it.

Briefly write the story of your trauma. Did it happen when you were a child? An adult? Did the event happen one time or many times? How long ago was the traumatic event, or when did ongoing trauma begin? Write this story as if you are a reporter—include just the facts and only the facts.

Trauma can have many elements. Describe any physical trauma or abuse you may have experienced. Include any details alongside your description: who, what, when, and so forth.

List any childhood neglect you may have experienced. You might have many examples, or you may have nothing to report. Neglect is when a parent does not provide a child with necessary food, clothing, shelter, supervision, or medical care, resulting in potential or actual harm. You may wish to also include any parental addictions here.

Explore emotional or psychological abuse you may have encoun-
tered. This type of abuse is very broad and could include such
experiences as inappropriate insults, bullying, harassment,
threats, intimidation, humiliation, isolation, extreme rules that
left you with little margin for success, or being ignored. Describe a
memory or two of any emotional trauma you experienced.

I am many wonderful things:
human, daughter, son,
child, mother, father, parent,
sister, brother, sibling, friend,
worker, volunteer, survivor.
I can keep my trauma
"right-sized" in reference
to all of who I am.

Have you ever watched someone else being abused? Maybe a sibling, parent, or friend? Have you ever been an observer of a crime where the victim feared for their life? Write about any types of trauma you may have observed.

If you have been the victim of intimate partner violence, whether it be physical, sexual, or psychological, write about your experience. This can be particularly painful to write about, so just add the details you feel comfortable with, or simply name the trauma and move on.

Describe any reactions you may have when you think about the traumas that have happened to you. Do you experience memories that feel like they come out of the blue? Reflect on how these experiences impact you. Do you become numb? Dysregulated? Start to explore this with any words that make sense to you.

When I feel fear or anxiety, I will remind myself how brave I have been in getting through the difficulties in my life. I will focus on my strengths and feel more respect for myself each day.

Do you tend to avoid memories of your trauma? Maybe you avoid memories of places you've lived or worked, or people you know. Do you avoid feelings associated with past trauma, such as sadness or anger? Write about these emotions or memories that you avoid.

_____

_____

_____

_____

_____

_____

_____

_____

_____

_____

_____

_____

_____

_____

_____

_____

_____

_____

_____

_____

_____

Do you tend to avoid certain places, people, or activities because they remind you of past trauma? Do you feel as though your life is smaller because of these avoidances? Perhaps you stopped going to places with crowds, or you no longer regularly hang out with friends. Reflect on these kinds of consequences here.

Do you have negative beliefs about yourself, others, or the world due to your trauma? These might be in the form of thoughts such as "I am broken" and "People are not safe," or statements having to do with personal expectations: "I need to be perfect" or "The world should stop harming me." Can you make connections between this thinking style and the time period after the trauma happened?

Do you blame yourself—or others—for the trauma you experienced? If so, does that make it hard for you to trust other people? Alternatively, do you feel less connected to other people because of your trauma? Write about your experience with blame, disconnection, trust, and detachment.

Do you feel that you are as involved with and excited about regular activities, such as social get-togethers, vacations, hobbies, or family outings, as you were before your trauma? Do you remember a time in your life when you regularly looked forward to various activities? Reflect on how it feels to deal with this shift in enjoyment.

Add Some Pleasure

Exploring your trauma will be challenging at times. Taking breaks, especially when the work becomes overwhelming, is a useful and important strategy to renew your energy so that you can refocus and keep moving forward.

To build a habit of giving yourself opportunities for renewal, make a list of pleasurable activities that you have participated in in the past, and those you practice now. This could include hobbies, little indulgences, time with friends, learning new things, or unstructured relaxing... whatever it is that you enjoy. If trauma has kept you from indulging in recreation, it may be necessary to figure out what works for you. Ask friends and family for ideas or reminders of fun things you used to do.

Once you have a useful list, you can work on determining which activities seem to be most effective for recentering when you feel specific strong emotions. What helps you stay present and regulated? What can you do as a transitional activity, to move from doing some trauma work to returning to your regular life endeavors?

If you can remember clearly what your life was like before the trauma, would you describe your emotions as similar, or definitely different? What are the feelings that seem to predominate since the trauma happened? Do you feel more irritable, for example? Angry? Overwhelmed? Negative? Choose a couple of emotions and write about your before and after experiences.

Have you had on-and-off problems with sleep since your trauma? What is the current quality of your sleep? How many hours do you get on an average night? Do you have a hard time falling and/or staying asleep? Do you occasionally have nightmares? Do you feel like you get quality sleep? Describe your overall sleep situation.

Prepare Your Brain for Sleep

In order to take this trek toward recovery, you need to bring your best. That means you need your brain to be in the best condition possible to facilitate change. Restful sleep allows your brain to heal, consolidate memories, and make sense of patterns in your life. Developing a better sleeping practice may take time, but it can be a game changer.

A powerful strategy for better sleep is to improve your "sleep hygiene," a catchall term for the actions we take to ensure restful sleep. These include keeping the temperature of the room comfortable, choosing comfortable bedding, eliminating light sources, keeping to a regular schedule, and avoiding specific foods and drinks—as well as phone and computer screens—too close to bedtime.

Adopting some good pre-sleep habits, like a ritual of reading, stretching, meditation, or journaling, can train your body and brain to relax, slow down, and drift into sleep. Learn more about sleep hygiene from your doctor and experiment with a pre-sleep routine.

Reflect on your support system, the people who are there for you when the going gets tough. Do you feel you've had good support since you experienced your trauma? Describe the quality of the support you have in your life and how it's changed. If you do not have good support, write about what seems to be missing.

Gather Your Support System

Our support systems provide us with understanding, empathy, guidance, mentoring, normalization, and even physical help. While you seek to understand yourself in reference to your trauma, you may find yourself in need of others to help you make sense of what you're learning. You may need insight about what your symptoms look like to other people. You may need to talk about your strong feelings. And sometimes you might need a hug, a shoulder to cry on, or a pat on the back.

Are there people in your life who can provide things you need? Have you lost touch with friends, family, or others you can rely on? Attend to your relationships and make sure you have two or three people in your support system who are willing to talk with you when you're struggling.

Also consider making therapy part of your support system. You might have some difficulty sharing very private details about your trauma with family or friends, because you believe it might harm them or that it will not be helpful. Check with your health insurance provider to find out your options for therapy. If you do not have health insurance, many therapists offer a sliding-scale fee that can be adjusted based on your income. You can also contact the National Alliance on Mental Illness (NAMI) HelpLine for additional information and referrals to various treatment services.

Summarize how you see yourself right now, at the beginning of this journey. What metaphor seems most appropriate to describe your thoughts and feelings? Are you about to climb a mountain, enter a dark forest, or sail a boat across a stormy sea? What roadblocks or barriers do you think might get in your way? And what will you do to remove them?

Close your eyes and imagine yourself as a healed person. What will your thinking be like? What will you tell yourself about your experience as a trauma survivor? In what ways would you think differently about yourself if you were healed, compared to now? Write with as much detail as you wish.

Continue to imagine yourself as a healed person. What are your feelings like? What feelings do you think will dominate your sense of self at the completion of your healing journey? Describe what it's like to feel so differently about yourself. Include as many feelings as you would like.

As you imagine yourself as a healed person, what are your behaviors like? What actions and activities are part of your healed self? How frequently will you be doing these things? When, where, how? Write down as many details as you think will be helpful.

Each step I take moving forward in my life is evidence that I care about myself. I will notice and celebrate each action I take to heal myself. I will be grateful for every effort.

Set Goals for This Work

Setting good goals makes it possible to know you are headed in the right direction. With some online research, you'll find many approaches and formats for goal-setting that you can try. No matter which method you use, here's some universal guidance:

Write it down. Post your goal somewhere you will see it daily. Make sure each step toward your goal has a measurable action (or several!) attached. For example, "Expand my support system" might include "Invite a friend to coffee to catch up and reconnect."

Talk about it. Tell other people about your goal. Ask for support. Take the journey with someone else who has a similar goal so that you can support each other and remind yourselves why you set your goals.

Feel it deeply. Regularly review your efforts. Let yourself get excited about any progress. Incorporate regular rewards for positive behaviors.

Recommit daily. Make sure you don't go more than one day without taking some sort of action toward your goal.

Identify roadblocks. Explore and own any ways you tend to sabotage your goals. Give this information to someone in your support system to help you.

I will regularly connect to the person I know I can become. I will allow a sense of excitement to envelop me as I think about being healed, whole, wiser, and more aware.

Set a specific goal for yourself based on what you believe you could be thinking, feeling, and doing as a healed trauma survivor. Read back through the previous prompts in which you imagined yourself at the end of your journey. Deeply connect to what your life could look like. Write a few sentences to that future self, letting them know how excited you are to meet them.

Thoughts, Feelings, and Sensations

Working on your trauma can feel like peeling an onion. After the initial layers of acknowledging the type of trauma, exploring your reactions since the experience, and deciding on some goals to move you forward, you will begin to work on the next layers of thoughts, feelings, and physical sensations. Understanding these deeper layers will help you better recognize triggers and identify (and overcome) self-defeating behaviors.

Your emotions will be your clearest indicators of the areas you need to focus on, and they'll help you recognize when you are doing better. Emotions are usually preceded by a thought or two, so noticing these and correcting any distortions in thinking can be vital. Thoughts and feelings can lead us to healthy actions—and to self-defeating behaviors. Understanding how to manage them enables you to set your course in a positive direction.

For some trauma survivors, the data that the body provides is easier for them to access, and make sense of, compared to their feelings. However, feelings and reactions to trauma are both held in the body. For example, the body can indicate the strength of a stress reaction through tension in the shoulders. A sick stomach might mean you are anxious. Learning your personal signals can help you determine a plan to address whatever's behind them.

When you have more awareness of your emotions, and their connection to physical systems, it becomes possible to connect them to their precipitants, or *triggers*. Triggers frequently take the form of a current experience that feels similar to something experienced during the original trauma. Triggers might be sounds, feelings, people, places, smells, or even a particular time of the year. Expanding your knowledge of triggers can help you intervene to prevent a trigger from overwhelming you.

I can become more and more comfortable with all emotions related to my trauma, knowing they can provide useful information to help me grow. I will accept emotions as gifts.

Soothing Strong Emotions

When we feel strong emotions, we don't always act in ways that are congruent with our value system. One useful self-soothing technique that you can use anywhere is to focus on your senses. Try this 5-4-3-2-1 exercise when you feel your emotions are over-powering you.

5: Sit comfortably if you can. Take a deep breath, and breathe out slowly. Notice any five objects that are near you. As you continue to breathe slowly and deeply, rest your eyes on each in turn, and observe the color, shape, size, purpose, and other qualities of each object.

4: Next, continuing with your controlled breathing, turn your attention to four physical sensations of your choice. Notice your feet pressing against the floor; feel your back against your chair.

3: Then, touch three things that are within your immediate reach. Choose surfaces that have different textures (rough, smooth, bumpy, etc.) and notice the sensation of each. Continue to breathe deeply.

2: Now, listen for two different sounds, whatever they may be. Notice the differences. Breathe.

1: Finish by taking one deep breath through your nostrils, and observe any scents that come to your awareness. Sit quietly, breathing and relaxing, for as long as you need to.

Think back to three recent experiences when you became angry. Relive each in your imagination, with as much detail as you can. Reflect on these experiences with anger. Where do you feel anger in your body? What do you do when you're angry? Describe your anger with an analogy or metaphor. Do you simmer with rage, boil over, or explode?

Continue to focus on the feeling of anger. Can you identify any specific thoughts you had during these recent experiences? What was the tone of your thoughts? Were you hypercritical, irrational, hurtful? What about speed—were your thoughts frantic and out of control? Write out any thoughts that come to mind. Are there any that seem extreme or problematic?

Mentally rewind the last day or week and notice any triggers or events that happened earlier that made you angry or made you experience anger. These could be things that reminded you of your trauma, or times when you were unable to get enough sleep, when you felt sick, or when you were dealing with too much stress.

Consider the totality of your experience with anger. Do you notice any patterns? Are the events that trigger or lead to anger similar? Do you react predictably? If you don't notice any patterns, try journaling about new anger experiences as they come up, until you have enough data for patterns to emerge. Are your triggers becoming clear?

I will create space in my life to self-evaluate on a daily basis. I will celebrate every effort I make to understand and transform myself. I will note any challenges and commit to change.

Explore another emotion, such as fear/anxiety, irritability, numbness/boredom, depression, or guilt/shame. Reflect on your experiences with this emotion. Where do you feel it in your body? What do you do with it? Describe it with an analogy or metaphor.

Continue to focus on the feeling you selected in the previous prompt. Can you identify any specific thoughts you had during these recent experiences? What was the tone of your thoughts? Were you hypercritical, irrational, hurtful? What about speed— were your thoughts frantic and out of control? Write out any thoughts that come to mind. Are there any that seem extreme or problematic?

Mentally rewind the last day or week and notice any triggers or events that happened earlier that made you emotionally vulnerable or made you experience this emotion. These could be things that reminded you of your trauma, or times when you were unable to get enough sleep, when you felt sick, or when you were dealing with too much stress.

Consider the totality of your experience with this emotion. Do you notice any patterns? Are the events that trigger or lead to this emotion similar? Do you react predictably? If you don't notice any patterns, try journaling about new experiences with this emotion as they come up, until you have enough data for patterns to emerge. Are your triggers becoming clear?

I can learn to be an unbiased observer of my trauma patterns. I will gain knowledge from myself and remain curious rather than judgmental so I can overcome patterns that are no longer useful.

Explore another emotion you haven't yet written about. Just as before, use this space to reflect on your experiences with this emotion. Where is it commonly felt in your body? Does it move through your body or stay in one place? What happens when it surfaces, and what do you do with it? Try to describe it with an analogy or metaphor.

Use this space to continue focusing on the feeling you selected in the previous prompt. What were some of the thoughts you had during the experiences where this feeling surfaced? Were they self-critical, confusing, worrisome? Did they arrive suddenly and fade away quickly, or did they take up room and linger for a while? Are there any that seemed extreme or problematic?

Mentally rewind the last day or week and notice any triggers or events that happened earlier that made you emotionally vulnerable or made you experience this emotion. These could be things that reminded you of your trauma, or times when you were unable to get enough sleep, when you felt sick, or when you were dealing with too much stress.

Consider the totality of your experience with this emotion. Do you notice any patterns? Are the events that trigger or lead to this emotion similar? Do you react predictably? If you don't notice any patterns, try journaling about new experiences with this emotion as they come up, until you have enough data for patterns to emerge. Are your triggers becoming clear?

The goal of understanding your triggers is to find ways to effectively anticipate negative reactions before they happen, or prevent or avoid specific triggering situations. As you journal about your emotions, think about and describe any specific sounds or smells that tend to upset you for a time after you are exposed to them. What do you notice about these types of triggers? Are they connected to your trauma? (We'll consider other trigger types in future prompts.)

A Mind/Body Scan for Healing

Learning to pay attention to the information your body and mind provide you will empower you to change dysfunctional habits—the unhelpful behaviors that are roadblocks on your healing journey. A mind/body scan is a simple but effective way to tune into the signals you might otherwise miss.

To start, sit or lie down and make yourself comfortable. First, notice the speed and nature of your thoughts. Allow your thoughts to rise and fade in your mind, noticing them without engaging with them. Are they negative? Curious? Frantic? Take note and let your thoughts float past you.

Next, switch your attention to focusing on your body. Start with your feet. What do you feel? Are they relaxed? Tense? Tired? Sore? Continue to scan up your body, to your legs, hips, stomach, arms, chest, shoulders, neck, mouth, eyes, and forehead. Note any thoughts or sensations that arise, and if you get distracted, gently return to your scanning.

To finish, try to connect any data you gathered from observing your mind to the sensations you detected in your body.

Think about any types of touch or physical closeness that you feel uncomfortable with—touch that you think should feel good or comforting but that largely upsets you. Can you make any connections between these types of triggers and your trauma? Reflect on some of these experiences and write about any connections you notice.

Consider things you can see that might be a trigger for a trauma reaction. For example, are you bothered by certain types of movies or television shows? Do certain physical attributes, like a particular hair color or body type, make you feel upset? Write about anything that you think could be a visual trigger.

Explore any situational triggers that may have parallels to your original trauma. Do you feel uncomfortable when you're around certain people, places, or things? Note these triggers and describe where, when, and how they affect you. Add to this list any time you react to a new situation, in case it could be related to a trigger.

Connecting Thoughts to Feelings

It's important to recognize that under most circumstances, thoughts precede feelings. To explore this, consider the example scenarios on this page and identify what you might think, and as a result, what you might feel, in each situation. Notice how the thought directly creates the feeling.

You're driving on the freeway, and someone in front of you suddenly changes lanes and cuts you off.

You think: *(Example: "That person had no regard for my safety. I almost hit that car.")*

Then you feel: *(Angry. Nervous.)*

Someone in your family asks you to do a big, inconvenient favor for them at the very last minute.

You think: ....

Then you feel: ....

Your boss praises several people for completing a project you all worked on, but doesn't mention you at all.

You think: ....

Then you feel: ....

You happen to see an ex with their new love interest.

You think: ....

Then you feel: ....

Your train experiences unexpected delays and you're late for work.

You think: ....

Then you feel: ....

Someone you are very close to lets you know they have cancer.

You think: ....

Then you feel: ....

You've just brought home a new desk from a furniture store, but when you start to assemble it, you cannot find your screwdriver.

You think: ....

Then you feel: ....

An expensive product you bought recently goes missing and you can't find it anywhere.

You think: ....

Then you feel: ....

Is stress a particular trigger for you? Do you react much more strongly to a stressor than seems reasonable? Reflect on different stressors that you tend to overreact to. Make a list and write about any connections to prior trauma. Keep in mind that a stressor might be a vulnerability, like lack of sleep, rather than a trigger.

Do you have any recurring negative behaviors or reactions to stress that you or someone close to you have noticed? Describe these behaviors and note any feelings, triggers, and vulnerabilities you think they may be connected to. Include any additional aspects of these behaviors, such as people, the time of day, etc.

My emotions are separate from my behavior. I can feel strongly without acting out in ways that are harmful to myself or my relationships. I can allow myself time to think before I act.

Interview for Insight

If you have trouble teasing out your patterns or behaviors, discuss them with a close friend, family member, spouse, or coworker who will be honest about what they've observed. Interview someone who knew you before you experienced your trauma, if possible. Ask questions like:

- Do you notice anything different about me since my trauma?

- Do I seem to show more of some emotions than I used to? Which ones?

- Have you observed me behaving differently than how I used to act? Give me some examples.

- Do you feel like we connect the way we used to? Do I focus on different topics in conversations? Do I seem more negative? Please share any details.

- Are there things I say or do that bother you or concern you? Give me some examples.

- Do I seem to avoid certain topics, activities, or other things?

Explore the consequences that you've noticed are paired with your negative behaviors. Who suffers as a result of these behaviors? You? Family? Workmates? Also write about any secondary gains you might get from acting out, such as people not demanding as much from you or being left alone to do what you want.

Look Back

Read what you wrote in section 1 about how you'll behave after
you're healed (see page 43). What will you need to work on first
to make that behavior a reality? Are there small actions you can
take now that could move you toward your goal? Make a list of
small, positive habits you can start working on.

A Healthy Time-Out

Sometimes it's hard to disengage from a heated situation. But taking a temporary time-out is a very healthy and important skill for anyone. Letting people know you are going to be briefly out of touch is a strong signal that you're actively working on yourself. Taking a time-out has three basic steps:

1. **Announce your time-out.** Tell whoever's directly involved what you're doing and how much time you'll need to calm down. Or, if it's not safe to be that open, simply excuse yourself and leave the area. In most cases, it takes at least 30 minutes to truly switch your brain's stress response from "activated" to "calm."

2. **Self-soothe with whatever works for you.** You might try a distracting activity like watching TV, a body-connecting activity like taking a walk, or a logic activity like writing down your thoughts and feelings. Avoid replaying the incident in your head, which will merely intensify the emotion.

3. **Return and re-engage.** If you are not calmed down, let the other party know you need more time.

I will look at my behaviors
and notice any consequences,
both obvious and subtle.
I can change negative
behaviors related to past
trauma. I can heal myself and
improve my relationships.

Healthy Body and Mind

We all experience stress, which affects us physically, emotionally, and behaviorally. Being aware of what causes stress can help us figure out ways to eliminate some stressors, minimize others, and change our psychological relationship with others still. None of us will be able to create a stress-free life. But we can develop a healthier relationship with stress by learning to counter our reactions to it. Employing healthy self-care is how we do just that.

Self-care is not selfish. Indeed, it can be argued that self-care is probably the most selfless thing you can do! Why? Because if you take good care of yourself, you become much more available to others. You can be a model of what it looks like to be healthy. And investing in a self-care routine will prevent you from losing big chunks of time trying to recover from out-of-control stress.

Self-care falls into two general categories: foundational and targeted. Foundational self-care includes necessary, often daily, self-care practices that create a healthy foundation so you can approach life at your best. Examples include getting proper sleep, eating right, exercising, being aware of stress, and maintaining social connections.

Targeted self-care is usually specific to a particular situation or problem. I picture it as a closet shelf filled with various bins and boxes that I can choose from to help me deal with whatever challenge comes my way. Targeted self-care works best when we have a wide variety of practices available to us, along with the awareness to determine what works.

I will discover and practice many ways to relax and recenter. I will give myself permission to slow down and see value in emotional and physical recovery.

Your Safe Place

This relaxation technique can be a valuable and versatile tool for your self-care.

First, sit or lie down in a comfortable position. Imagine you're in a place where you feel happy, calm, and safe. This might be a real place or one you make up. Look around in your mind's eye. What do you see? Picture as many details as possible.

Next, listen for sounds in your safe place. If you're on a beach, hear the waves and seagulls. If you're in your grandmother's kitchen, hear the fridge humming.

Now take a deep breath in your safe place and call to mind its scents. Do you smell the fragrances of grass or leaves, the smokiness of a fireplace?

Imagine any nearby textures that you can feel—the breeze on your skin, the sand under your feet.

Finally, notice how it feels to be in your safe place. Focus on your breathing, how relaxed your muscles feel, the quietness of your mind, and feeling happy, content, and peaceful. To finish, take three very deep breaths before you return to your regular activities.

What have you noticed to be your biggest stressors? Work? Family? Trauma? Pressure to succeed? List as many as you can. Describe the who, what, when, where, and how of your stress, and be as comprehensive as possible. Include any behaviors, circumstances, places, and memories that cause stress for you.

Return to the stressors you listed in the previous prompt and mark each one for any of the following qualities: "A" for an acute stressor that has a clear end, "C" for a chronic stressor that lingers and has no clear endpoint, "S" for a self-imposed stressor via pressure you put on yourself or poor choices, and "T" for a stressor caused or exacerbated by trauma.

Did any of these surprise you? Reflect on this here.

Change can be perceived as either good or bad, but will always feel stressful. What are some major changes you have experienced in the last 10 years? List and designate each change as either good or bad. Further mark each one as either actively chosen (like a divorce) or chosen for you by someone or by circumstance (like being fired from your job).

Do you know your stress limits? What are some of the cues that your stress level is too high? What are your physical and emotional responses to stress? Your behavioral responses? List as many of these responses as you can think of. Then write a commitment to notice specific signals of stress and to counter your stress with an act of self-care.

I will pay attention to my emotional, physical, and behavioral responses to stress. When my stress is too high, I will take care of myself in healthy, consistent ways.

Many healthy people regularly review their stressors and commit to eliminating or minimizing any stress that's crept in but has no value. For example, your Wednesdays might be hectic because after work you have to get to your book club . . . which you don't actually enjoy. Have you ever eliminated a stressor? Have you worked to minimize a stressor? Describe the experience and include any takeaways you learned about yourself.

Look Back

Review what you wrote about your trauma triggers in section 2 (starting on page 57). Which of your triggers feels most stressful to you? Which of your symptoms feel most difficult to handle? What do you now realize about how stress and trauma interact?

Getting good sleep will help you manage your stress and reduce trauma symptoms. Describe your normal sleep routine. Does it look the same every night? How many hours of sleep do you get? What actions do you take in the hour before bed? What activities seem to help you sleep? What seems to make your sleep worse?

Do you have nightmares? Write about any recurring themes you experience. What do you feel during the nightmares? What happens in your dreams? Who is present? Are there specific locations? If nightmares are a problem, consider keeping a separate journal to log your dreams, and note any connections to current stress you're experiencing.

I will commit to taking care of my body. I will embrace sleep, exercise, and eating right in order to create a healthy foundation for my recovery.

Write about your relationship with exercise. Do you exercise regularly, occasionally, or not at all? If you do, what do you notice about your stress level when you exercise? What do you tell yourself about exercise—do you think largely positive thoughts, or do you emphasize how hard it is? What are some rewards you've noticed from exercising? Describe as many as possible.

Eating right is part of foundational self-care and a reflection of your self-worth. Write about your relationship to food as if food were a person. What parts of the relationship are healthy? What parts of the relationship are difficult or even abusive? Make a commitment to yourself to improve this relationship.

LOOK BACK

Review what you wrote in section 1 about what your life will be like as a healed person (see pages 41–43). Describe what your sleep, exercise, and eating will be like when you're in that place of health and healing. Emphasize the emotional goodness of that transformation.

Do you have a person or two in your life who can help you with your trauma? Write out a short list of behaviors or symptoms that seem to be present when you are not doing very well. What are some ways that others could help you better manage those behaviors?

Good social support is necessary for our overall well-being. Write out any insights you have about your social support network. Do you have good friends? An ally at work? Good interactions with family? What needs are met by these people in your network? What needs might be unmet?

Forming Healthy Habits

Any task you can reduce to a habit will become easier and easier to accomplish. Forming a habit has three basic steps:

The cue: First, you must set up a cue, some external signal that will prompt the new behavior. A cue could be a specific time of the day, doing tasks in a particular order, being in a certain place, doing the behavior with the same people, or sometimes an emotion—performing the behavior when you feel a certain way.

The reward: Figure out a reward for the new behavior, like streaming a movie on days when you go to the gym. Once the new routine becomes established, you'll notice a deeper reward, such as feeling proud of yourself or having more energy.

The craving: Once the habit becomes firmly established, you'll find that you're internally motivated to do the routine.

Having regular fun is essential for a healthy life. What sort of activities do you like to take part in? Make a list. When was the last time you did them? Are you able to regularly schedule time for fun, or do you feel your life is too full of tasks and work? Describe your relationship with fun, and commit to improving it.

People with good communication skills find it easier to self-advocate, ask for help, and deepen their connections with others. Evaluate your own communication skills. What are your strengths? What are your areas of challenge? Are you better at listening or talking? What is one goal you can work toward to improve this?

Putting a positive spin on life's challenges is another form of self-care. Think of two difficulties you have gone through this past year, and describe them as you would to a friend. Then rewrite them with more positive wording that emphasizes your growth, what you learned, and your strengths.

Return to Baseline

Recognizing and adjusting your stress level is an important skill to develop. This includes improving how long it takes you to return to baseline.

Baseline is your status when your heart rate, thinking, and responses are at a normal, calm, and centered state. If calming down takes you a very long time, it will be vital to develop better skills to shorten that process. Take note next time you're in an agitating situation. Your heart rate will increase, your breathing will quicken, and you will have some strong thoughts, all very rapidly. At the beginning of that experience, note the time. Utilize some relaxation techniques described in this book, such as deep breathing (page 54), mindfulness (page 118), or the safe place activity (page 90).

If you're able to return to a normal heart rate and slowed breathing within 10 to 30 minutes, your self-soothing skills are up to the task. If not, try practicing relaxation skills much more regularly.

Learning to relax is an important part of your self-care. List the activities you find most relaxing. Determine a personal template for relaxation: describe what helps you relax, and when, how, and where it happens.

Increasing spiritual and mindfulness practices can add to your overall well-being. Do you read? Write daily gratitude lists? Belong to a faith-based community or organization? Practice meditation or mindfulness? Talk with like-minded people? Reflect on how these practices might enhance your life.

I will learn how to pair my self-care with my challenges. I will become aware of the many kinds of self-care I can put in my mental closet to access when needed.

Focus on the Positive

If you want to increase any behavior that you feel will be life-enhancing, focus on all of the positive aspects of that action. Write a list of all the good that will come from making this change, from helpful thoughts and feelings to supportive actions and good consequences. Look at the list daily. Become emotionally attached to how good it will feel. This will motivate you to do more.

The opposite is also true. If you want to stop a harmful behavior, like drinking too much alcohol, write a list of all the negative aspects of that choice. Describe how this behavior has caused problems for you and how it's made you feel bad, think more negatively, and/or make poor choices. Bring the list to mind to help deter you from repeating this behavior.

Look Back

Re-evaluate the self-defeating behaviors you wrote about in section 2 (starting from page 51). Are there any that you can identify as attempts at self-care? What did you believe the behaviors were trying to fix? Can you think of any new behaviors that might accomplish that goal in a healthier way?

Some people find that attending therapy to heal from trauma is one of the most important aspects of self-care. Write your thoughts and feelings about therapy here. Do you have any past experiences that color your feelings? If you were to attend therapy, what would your goals be? What qualities would you want the therapist to have?

Mindfulness for Self-Acceptance

Mindfulness techniques include a wide variety of exercises. One useful mindfulness practice is self-acceptance.

To practice mindful self-acceptance, bring to mind a recent experience when you made a mistake or acted out in some way that you feel was not reflective of your best self. With this fully in mind, talk to yourself as if you are a loving friend:

Tell yourself that you are learning and growing. Remind yourself of how far you have come.

Give yourself some helpful advice about what to try next.

Consider any funny aspects of the experience.

Emphasize that you are human, that you will make mistakes, and that you will always work toward better behavior.

The key to cultivating self-acceptance is to learn to avoid any sort of put-down, cruel self-criticism, name-calling, or abuse toward yourself. Use this self-acceptance exercise every time you do not like your behavior.

I can take care of myself with gentleness and respect. I will treat myself with the same loving attitude that I'd offer a dear friend or family member.

Growing and Thriving

I hope that you've come to recognize that writing in this journal is just the beginning of an exciting new path to recovery, healing, and growth. You'll find that learning new skills will help you figure out new directions to explore as you seek more knowledge. And even after you reach the place of healing you envisioned at the beginning of this book, you can continue exploring. Think of yourself as a traveler who will always be journeying somewhere to gain more insight.

Where will you go? Trust yourself to set the itinerary. One part of your journey may bring you toward an understanding that you deserve happiness, pleasure, and security. You may strive toward increased self-awareness to figure out what you like and dislike, what impedes your progress, and what opens you up to new possibilities. You may focus on learning to set better boundaries with yourself and others. Or you may find it necessary to set a course to go even deeper and explore your values to understand how they drive your decisions and goals.

Trauma does not define who you are. Healing and growth are absolutely possible after trauma. Moving forward is completely up to you, and I hope the topics we've discussed will help you get there. Learn and practice self-compassion, as it will help you during difficult parts of your trek. Tap into your personal support system for comfort, and for a different perspective on your experiences. Consider personal therapy to increase your ongoing progress. Keep moving forward. You are worth it!

I will continue to work on myself on a regular basis. I can appreciate each new gain in any area of my life. Growth will become a familiar friend.

Check-In Checklist

The next time you're feeling really good, centered, and healthy—which I hope will be very soon—pause and take a mental snapshot. Create a personal checklist of what goes on when you're well. What's happening with your foundational self-care, your sleep, exercise, eating, stress awareness, and so on? What about your social life? Your primary relationships? How are you dealing with your day-to-day stressors?

List the areas of your life that you feel are going right, in detail. Include any relevant thoughts, feelings, and behaviors. Anytime that you feel you aren't doing well, you can refer to this checklist and consider which areas of your life are still dialed in, and which you're struggling with. Then set goals to get back on track.

Write about your relationship with self-judgment. Outline areas of yourself that you tend to judge harshly, with particular emphasis on your trauma experience. These may be "I statements" that you tell yourself ("I am healing too slow." "I can't stand how I feel."), or they might be observations ("Avoiding social situations makes me feel like a loser.").

Counter the self-judgments with self-compassionate responses. Think of how a loving friend would talk to you when you are struggling. For example, "I am healing a little each day. I am managing my emotions minute by minute." Write down your compassionate statements and read them to yourself daily for one week.

What makes you truly happy? Do you feel happy when you're working on improving yourself or when practicing new skills? Does experiencing growth light you up? Are loving relationships the key? Reflect on what you recognize about your own paths to happiness.

Do you pay attention to small, pleasant moments? Is it easy for you to slow down and notice the good things in your everyday life, or do you rush through your days? Describe some small, mundane pleasures you've noticed and appreciated. How can you improve this awareness going forward?

I will try to pay attention to life's pleasures and be aware of what I like and dislike. I will choose to notice the happy moments and celebrate them, big and small.

Perform an internet search for a list of core values and pick the three that are most important to you. Envision how they serve as guiding stars to keep you from drifting off course. Describe how these values have helped you in your life, including at work and in your relationships.

Pick three additional values that are also important to you. Describe how these values have helped you in your life.

After reflecting on your values, review some of the major decisions and choices you made during the previous week. Take note if any were driven by your values. Was it easier for you to make these choices? Did the decisions flow out of someplace deep within you? Describe what it is like to make value-driven choices.

Next, look back on any choices you have made recently that disappointed you. Review a choice or two and write about any barriers that kept you from making a value-driven choice. Did someone else's values get in the way? Did you abandon yourself for some reason?

I will learn from the decisions, choices, and consequences in my life, and will continue to gain insight from them.
I will strive to live a value-driven life.

Boundaries between ourselves and others are also driven by our values. One of the core tenets of boundaries is emotional safety. What kinds of behaviors, attitudes, or actions from others make you feel safe? What makes you feel unsafe? Describe both situations. Write about your relationship to emotional safety and reflect on ways you can improve it.

Healthy people keep some aspects of their story private. What are your rules for sharing details of your trauma? Are your rules clear and easy to adhere to, or do you tend to play it by ear? Outline your rules, including the who, what, when, where, and how.

All of us make mistakes, big and small. Upholding our values and having criteria for forgiving our mistakes is necessary for healing and moving forward. Describe your mechanism for self-forgiveness, especially when you feel you didn't meet your values. If you don't have a process, talk with some close friends and formulate a new practice.

The journey with trauma will be lifelong, with new challenges that may require new skills. When you find yourself hitting a wall with your recovery, how will you expand your skill set to move forward? What's one new skill you want to learn right now? What are some actions you can take to begin to master it?

Look Back

Now that you have explored so much, how would you describe yourself in regard to your trauma? Write several "I am" statements that detail new insights, awareness, and recognition. Be sure to touch on how far you have come, as well as where you believe you still need to go.

Setting Standards

Our values can guide us and serve as anchors to make sure we hold fast to ourselves through the twists and turns of life. However, we are all human, and rigid standards or striving for perfection makes it very difficult to live life. One way to avoid this pitfall is to define both a personal standard and a minimum standard. For example, a personal standard for fitness could be to work out six days a week, while a minimum standard could be to never go below three days per week. If you fall below your minimum standard, it should trigger a recommitment on your part.

Consider some areas of your life where you have been self-critical or regularly felt guilt or shame. See if establishing these two types of standards helps you practice self-compassion.

Look Back

If you've been writing in this journal for some time, describe your progress and what it's been like to explore your trauma. What have the highlights been? What's been your biggest takeaway? What was hardest for you? What areas do you feel need further attention?

Small changes can add up over time, eventually creating a substantial shift. What are some small, positive behaviors or habits you've acquired since you began writing about your trauma? List all of the gains, no matter how small. Take time to celebrate each gain.

Other people in your life are certainly impacted by your reactions to trauma and your healing. What have you noticed about your relationships with others since you began this process? Has anyone noticed you are working on yourself? Write about any comments or reactions from others related to your growth.

My Picture Gallery

Sometimes we get out of touch with our happiness and who we really know ourselves to be. To help you when you are feeling disconnected, create a picture gallery of who you are. You can do this on a poster board, on a cork board, or with your phone or digital device. Add pictures that reflect your true self: things you love, places you have traveled to, friends and family, activities, anything that has meaning for you. Be sure to include pictures of yourself from times when you feel connected and happy. Add meaningful sayings or favorite affirmations along with the images. Keep adding to the gallery as you notice new things that bring you pleasure.

Look at your gallery often to remind you of these important things and reconnect with what matters to you.

Growth may always feel somewhat uncomfortable, and so can actions that are unhealthy or wrong. Reflect on the "good" kind of uncomfortable that leads to growth, versus the "bad" kind of uncomfortable that is a signal to stop some behavior. How do you tell the difference? How do you stay in growth mode when you're feeling uncomfortable?

Look Back

Review the symptoms, triggers, emotions, and behaviors that
you have equated with your trauma. Have any of them shifted or
changed since you began this work? Describe any changes in your
symptoms, new awareness of triggers, better relationships with
emotions, and healthier behaviors.

I can set healthy boundaries with myself and others. I will allow my experiences to teach me when I need to make new boundaries to stay safe.

Have a Meeting with Yourself

Self-evaluation is an effective habit for anyone who wants to regularly move forward in their life. A useful way to do this is to regularly schedule a meeting with yourself to review goals, note progress, and commit to the next steps. Draw up a formal agenda for the meeting that meets your needs and your process. In the meeting, you could review your trauma symptoms, note any changes, and determine what to work on next. You could outline your self-care strategies and decide on areas that need improvement and attention. Ask yourself about any roadblocks and decide how you will overcome them. You may also want to take the time to deeply reflect on all of your progress, to allow that pleasure to motivate you to keep moving ahead.

Describe your experience with personal growth. Do you go through periods of working on yourself, then stop altogether? Or do you slowly but surely move forward? Touch on any changes that you want to incorporate to continue to move forward in your healing journey.

Since this is merely the beginning of overcoming your trauma, you will have more to learn and practice. What are your next steps? Where are you gaining traction? What areas feel like they are stalled or need more work? Write out a plan for the next steps in your recovery.

Write a Letter to Your Future Self

The journey through your trauma will change again and again. If you were to write your story in the immediate aftermath of a traumatic experience, it might center on the pain and confusion you feel. As you move on, the story can transform and change in ways that reflect your growth, insights, and new awareness. Write a letter to your future self about what you want that story to be. Detail how your symptoms have shifted. Review your previous writings about negative experiences and add any scenarios that you look forward to as your future self. Include details of how your future self feels about the strength in your vulnerability, how emotionally available you will be, shifts in self-compassion, and how self-reliant you have become. Finish the letter with appreciation and the meaning you have made from your healing journey.

I will practice self-compassion every day and treat myself as a loving friend. I will embrace my humanness and recognize that growth can be challenging and exciting.

RESOURCES

Below are a variety of resources you can use to aid you on your journey of healing from trauma. They include websites with educational resources, recommended books, a guide to finding apps and podcasts for additional support, and hotlines for treatment services.

Your health insurance provider can be a great resource for finding a therapist who specializes in trauma. Call their service number or check their online resource for a searchable list. Also ask friends and family for a therapist they recommend.

WEBSITES

NIMH.NIH.gov
The National Institute of Mental Health provides research and education for many mental health issues, including post-traumatic stress disorder (PTSD).

NAMI.org
The National Alliance on Mental Illness provides education and support for those dealing with mental health issues, and also provides family support in local chapters.

SuicidePreventionLifeline.org
The National Suicide Prevention Lifeline provides 24/7 support for anyone having suicidal thoughts. They also provide information for professionals, such as best practices for suicide response.

VTT.ovc.ojp.gov/what-is-vicarious-trauma
The Vicarious Trauma Toolkit is available to anyone who wants to learn more about secondary trauma.

ADAA.org/understanding-anxiety/posttraumatic-stress
-disorder-ptsd/resources
The Anxiety & Depression Association of America provides educational materials, along with a free monthly e-newsletter to help you stay abreast of new information about trauma, PTSD, anxiety, and depression.

www.PTSD.VA.gov
Information from the Veterans Affairs site is applicable to most trauma survivors.

HelpGuide.org/articles/ptsd-trauma/helping-someone
-with-ptsd.htm
This website compiles information and resources to help individuals with PTSD and those who love them.

https://www.psychologytoday.com/us/therapists
Psychology Today provides a robust directory of therapists, psychologists, and other mental health professionals that can be filtered by mental health issues, types of therapy, payment options, and more.

BOOKS

Van der Kolk, Bessel. *The Body Keeps the Score: Brain, Mind, and Body in the Healing of Trauma.* New York: Penguin, 2014.
One of the best books describing the ways PTSD manifests in the body.

Walker, Matthew P. *Why We Sleep: Unlocking the Power of Sleep and Dreams.* New York: Scribner, 2017.
The best book about sleep I have ever read. If sleep is your Achilles' heel, this book can help enormously.

APPS, PODCASTS, AND MORE

There are many free smartphone apps that were originally written for the military and include mindfulness and breathing exercises, along with mental health education and tracking. Search for apps created by the Department of Veterans Affairs or the Defense Health Agency.

Search your favorite podcast platform for PTSD- or trauma-related programs to learn more from professionals and survivors.

Innumerable apps, websites, and local classes are available to teach you valuable mindfulness skills. Try out different types to find the ones that best fit your needs and personality.

HOTLINES

NAMI HelpLine: 1-800-950-6264
The National Alliance on Mental Illness provides a complementary service that offers referrals to treatment services, information on mental health conditions, and support to family members and caregivers..

SAMHSA's National Helpline: 1-800-662-HELP (4357)
The Substance Abuse and Mental Health Services Administration offers another complementary service that can be used for treatment referrals and obtaining information for those with mental health disorders.

REFERENCES

American Psychiatric Association. *Diagnostic and Statistical Manual of Mental Disorders.* 5th ed. Washington, DC: American Psychiatric Publishing, 2013.

Aspy, Denholm J., and Michael Proeve. "Mindfulness and Loving-Kindness Meditation: Effects on Connectedness to Humanity and to the Natural World." *Psychological Reports* 120, no. 1 (January 2017): 102–17. doi.org/10.1177/0033294116685867.

Beck, Judith S. *Cognitive Behavior Therapy: Basics and Beyond.* 2nd ed. New York: Guilford Press, 2011.

Breslau, Naomi. "Epidemiologic Studies of Trauma, Posttraumatic Stress Disorder, and Other Psychiatric Disorders." *Canadian Journal of Psychiatry* 47, no. 10 (December 2002): 923–29. doi.org/10.1177/070674370204701003.

Chan, K. M., and K. Horneffer. "Emotional Expression and Psychological Symptoms: A Comparison of Writing and Drawing." *The Arts in Psychotherapy* 33, no. 1 (December 2006): 26–36. doi.org/10.1016/j.aip.2005.06.001.

Clear, James. *Atomic Habits: Tiny Changes, Remarkable Results.* New York: Avery, 2018.

Cloitre, Marylene, K. Chase Stovall-McClough, Kate Nooner, Patty Zorbas, Stephanie Cherry, Christie L. Jackson, Weijin Gan, and Eva Petkova. "Treatment for PTSD Related to

Childhood Abuse: A Randomized Controlled Trial." *American Journal of Psychiatry* 167, no. 8 (August 2010): 915–24. doi.org/10.1176/appi.ajp.2010.09081247.

Duhigg, Charles. *The Power of Habit: Why We Do What We Do in Life and Business.* New York: Random House, 2012.

Friedman, Matthew. J., Patricia A. Resick, Richard A. Bryant, and Chris R. Brewin. "Considering PTSD for DSM-5." *Depression and Anxiety* 28, no. 9 (September 2011): 750–69. doi.org /10.1002/da.20767.

Gilbert-Eliot, Trudy. *Healing Secondary Trauma: Proven Strategies for Caregivers and Professionals to Manage Stress, Anxiety, and Compassion Fatigue.* Emeryville, CA: Rockridge Press, 2020.

Koenen, Karestan C., and Sandro Galea. "Post-traumatic Stress Disorder and Chronic Disease: Open Questions and Future Directions." *Social Psychiatry and Psychiatric Epidemiology* 50, no. 4 (February 2015): 511–13. doi.org/10.1007/s00127-015 -1035-0.

Larner, Brad, and Adrian Blow. "A Model of Meaning-Making Coping and Growth in Combat Veterans." *Review of General Psychology* 15, no. 3 (September 2011): 187–97. doi.org/10.1037 /a0024810.

Lasiuk, G. C., and K. M. Hegadoren. "Posttraumatic Stress Disorder Part I: Historical Development of the Concept." *Perspectives in Psychiatric Care* 42, no. 1 (February 2006): 13–20. doi.org/10.1111/j.1744-6163.2006.00045.x.

Linehan, Marsha M. *DBT Skills Training Manual.* 2nd ed. New York: Guilford Press, 2015.

Olff, Miranda, Willie Langeland, Nel Draijer, and Berthold P. Gersons. "Gender Differences in Posttraumatic Stress Disorder." *Psychological Bulletin* 133, no. 2 (April 2007): 183–204. doi.org/10.1037/0033-2909.133.2.183.

Roberts, A. L., S. E. Gilman, J. Breslau, N. Breslau, and K. C. Koenen. "Race/Ethnic Differences in Exposure to Traumatic Events, Development of Post-Traumatic Stress Disorder, and Treatment-Seeking for Post-Traumatic Stress Disorder in the United States." *Psychological Medicine* 41, no. 1 (January 2011): 71–83. doi.org/10.1017/S0033291710000401.

Tedeschi, Richard G., Jane Shakespeare-Finch, Kanako Taku, and Lawrence G. Calhoun. *Posttraumatic Growth: Theory, Research, and Applications.* New York: Routledge, Taylor & Francis, 2018.

Van der Kolk, Bessel. *The Body Keeps the Score: Brain, Mind, and Body in the Healing of Trauma.* New York: Penguin, 2014.

Walker, Matthew P. *Why We Sleep: Unlocking the Power of Sleep and Dreams.* New York: Scribner, 2017.

Acknowledgments

Thank you to the great team at Rockridge Press for their professionalism and support. Gratitude to my parents for teaching me a work ethic that keeps me focused and moving forward. Deepest appreciation and love to all my children for the constant joy you bring to my life. Watching you interact as adults brings me great happiness. And for my sweetheart, Daryl, all my love for not holding me to my summer of "no." I am the luckiest woman alive.

About the Author

Trudy Gilbert-Eliot, PhD, LMFT, LCADC, is a licensed psychotherapist in Las Vegas, Nevada. She specializes in working with first responders and is a contractor with the Las Vegas Metropolitan Police Department. She has worked with trauma survivors throughout her 25-year career, including abused children, battered women, psychiatric patients, addicts, and alcoholics, and most recently with military personnel, veterans, and first responders. She has also provided psychological support for those impacted by critical incidents, including mass shootings, hostage situations, suicides, and armed robberies. Currently in private practice, she also teaches workshops on a variety of topics for the University of Nevada, Reno. She was recently featured on eight episodes of the CASAT Conversations podcast, providing guidance for family members of first responders.